Help Your Child T

Bad Bear

ALLAN AHLBERG and ERIC HILL

GRANADA
London Toronto Sydney New York

Help Your Child To Read

Parents can help their children to start reading. It is not difficult, nor is it necessary to be a trained teacher. In many ways home is a better place to start than school. In school your child will share the teacher's time with 25 or 30 others. At home he can have your undivided attention.

The series HELP YOUR CHILD TO READ is a set of books for parents to share with their children. The books contain stories, rhymes and games. Also, on page 3 of each book, there are practical suggestions for parents: ways in which they can help their children to start reading.

Golden Rules

Learning to read is not a tidy process. There is no royal road. However, there are a few points it's as well to bear in mind.

1 Avoid anxiety about your child's 'progress'. If you become anxious, so will the child. Children should learn that reading is entertaining and useful — not something to worry about.

2 Don't be in a hurry. Children start talking at different ages, and make progress at different rates. The same is true of reading.

3 Finally, don't overdo things. Ten minutes of shared reading or writing a day is ample. If the child loses interest, don't force him. Enjoyment is the key.

Beware of the bear

Who's been licking
my lolly?
Bad Bear!

Who's been kicking
my dolly?
Bad Bear!

Who hit the ducks
with a loaf of bread?
Bad Bear!

Who dropped a bucket on Poorly Pig's head?
Bad Bear!

And who's been sleeping in my bed?

Bad Bear!

Very Bad Bear

Here is Bad Bear

being bad.

Here is Bad Bear

being very bad.

Here is Bad Bear

being very very bad.

Here is Bad Bear

being sorry.

Here is Bad Bear

being good.

Here is Bad Bear

being very good.

Here is Bad Bear

being bad again.

Bad Bear's picnic

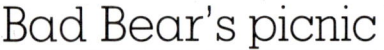

If you go down
to the woods today
don't let Bad Bear
see you.

She'll take your jelly
and cakes away
your crisps
and chocolate too.

She'll climb a tree
and gobble the lot
then even see
what else you have got
so please take care
don't let Bad Bear
surprise you.

Balancing bears

1 bear and 2 bears make 3 bears.

3 bears and 3 bears make 6 bears.

6 bears and 4 bears make 10 bears.

10 bears and Bad Bear make . . .

... too many bears!

Bye bye Bad Bear

When Bad Bear sleeps
it's understood
she's sometimes almost
nearly good.

Yet still she tries
sometimes it seems
to be a bad bear
in her dreams!

The end